by Tekla White * illustrated by Joe Boddy

MODERN CURRICULUM PRESS
Pearson Learning Group

The wind whined around the California hills one July morning in 1849, but no one worried about it. Caravans of miners (called "forty-niners") just kept coming. They kept panning for gold, hoping to strike it rich. They tried to hold on to their hats, but it didn't do any good. The wind snatched every last hat and sent them sailing down the hill. The miners didn't take time to run after their hats. They just kept sloshing the water and gravel around looking for glitter. If they found enough flakes of gold in their pans, they could buy all the hats in California.

Peggy Ann, who washed the laundry for the mining camp, hung the clothes out to dry on the bushes. The blankets flapped around like wings on a flock of geese.

"Mr. Wind, you sure woke up in an ugly mood," Peggy Ann said. "It won't bother me. You keep huffing and puffing and these white blankets will dry faster than a puddle of water on a hundred-degree day."

By lunchtime the wind was carrying on something frightful. It screamed through the branches of the oak trees, since no one else paid any attention. The trees just bowed, as if they were honoring their partners for a square dance.

The wind hooted through the canyons. Still, nobody paid any attention.

The wind sent tents soaring through the air. It turned the trees wrong side out. Everything not tied down flew right out of camp. Peggy Ann's white blankets went sailing up so high in the air that they caught on the mountain peaks. It looked as if it had snowed in the middle of summer. The wind even snatched the hair off a grizzly bear who was catching salmon for breakfast!

When the wind blew itself out of breath, Peggy Ann opened the door and peered outside. The wind had bundled up some of the clothes Peggy Ann had washed and had left them by her front door.

Peggy Ann picked up the first bunch of clothes and dropped it just as quick. The clothes wiggled and kicked and let out a big cry. Working its way out of a stack of shirts was an arm and a leg. Peggy Ann gently pulled the arm. A child not old enough to talk scrambled out of the laundry. When Peggy Ann picked the baby up, the fussing stopped. The baby cooed as sweetly as a dove. Right away she wrapped her smile around Peggy Ann's heart.

    No one knew who the baby was or where she belonged. The miners named her Baby Windy. They gave her some of their blankets so she'd stay warm at night. They carved a wooden cradle and made a basket of toys for her.

    Three days after the big wind, a caravan of pack mules trudged up the path. From a distance, they looked like a parade of ants carrying someone's picnic lunch. The mules were loaded down with supplies to sell to the miners. Some of the pans, picks, and shovels looked familiar to Peggy Ann. They were just like the ones the wind had carted off.

"Bandits," Peggy Ann said to Baby Windy. "This caravan is loaded down with everything that blew away in the wind. Nothing on these mules belongs to the mule drivers."

Peggy Ann saw her own two cows and her milking pails tied to the last mule. She tried to talk the bandits out of her cows, but they wouldn't give them back. While Peggy Anne was trying to convince the bandits, Baby Windy crawled to the cows, untied them, and led them behind the house. Then she went back for Peggy Ann's pails and the butter churn.

The bandits were in such a hurry to flee from Peggy Ann's sharp tongue that they didn't even notice anything was missing.

One day Peggy Ann went looking for Baby Windy. She discovered her milking the cows. After that, Peggy Ann didn't have to worry about getting milk. Whenever Baby Windy was thirsty, she went out to find the cows and helped herself to a pail or two of milk. Then she balanced the rest of the milk in a pail on her head and carried it home.

There were other advantages to having Baby Windy around. For one thing, she could blow as hard as the wind in a funnel cloud. She dried all the clothes as soon as Peggy Ann pulled them out of the tub. Then she blew them into stacks all neat and folded.

The next spring, the streams flooded. It looked as if the water would wash all the tents and Peggy Ann's cabin right down to Sacramento. Baby Windy saw what was happening and blew the water out of the way. The streams poured down the hills in one big river. All that water gave Sacramento a good washing. Everyone had to wade knee-deep through the city. They'd never heard about Baby Windy. They just figured too much melting snow caused the mess.

One morning not too long after that, a small earthquake rocked the hills. It felt like a mother rocking a cradle. Some miners were digging under the ground near Rattler's Gulch. The earthquake didn't amount to much, so they kept digging.

But the wild animals didn't like the earthquake. They stampeded over the top of the mine, trying to get as far away as they could. Their running made the ground bounce. All the posts holding up the roof in the mine fell over. Then the rocks in the ceiling came crashing down. The miners were trapped.

Peggy Ann, with Baby Windy in her arms, went running to the mine to see what had caused the commotion. While Peggy Ann talked to the other miners, Baby Windy crawled around looking the situation over.

As she crawled, Baby Windy heard the miners breathing and groaning below the ground. She found a soft spot in the ground and started blowing the dirt out of the way. Baby Windy tunneled down to the trapped miners. She crawled down the hole and led them out. All the while, Peggy Ann and the other miners were talking about what they should do.

On the way out of the collapsed mine, Baby Windy picked up a few gold nuggets. Her tunnel had run smack into the richest vein of gold in the Sierra foothills.

The five miners were mighty pleased when they saw the sky. They even picked up a fortune or two in gold on the way out. Everyone in camp marched down to Sacramento that night lugging a ton of gold nuggets.

Peggy Ann didn't need to do any more laundry. The miners were so wealthy now, they threw away their dirty clothes and bought new outfits. Peggy Ann thought it would be better to live in town anyway. When Baby Windy was old enough, she could go to school and learn to read and write.

In about a year Baby Windy started to walk. She didn't grow much taller, but she got stronger every day. Just to prove it, she picked up everything that wasn't fastened down—and some things that were! She loved animals more than anything else. They were always following her home. People knocked on Peggy Ann's door day and night to ask for their goats and their cattle. The people were frustrated. They joked that Windy was one of the worst bandits they'd ever known.

Peggy Ann didn't know what to do. Windy was hiding pigs in her closet and chickens under the bed. Pretty soon all the cats and dogs in the city were running around Peggy Ann's yard.

Peggy Ann scolded Windy and made her take everything back. Then Windy crawled up in Peggy Ann's lap and gave her a big kiss to say she was sorry. Peggy Ann's heart melted like a pound of butter in the hot July sun.

Windy had a streak of mischief in her too. She liked to blow the chimneys off houses. The bricks and stones were her favorite building blocks. People in Sacramento had a town meeting and said Windy had to go to Alaska or someplace far away. They wanted her exiled from their city. Windy asked for one more chance.

Windy tried to do good deeds for all the people in the town. She blew holes in the ground for people who needed well water. She blew away the rain clouds so there weren't any more storms. But there was just one drawback to that idea: without the rain, all the rivers dried up.

Everyone in town was angry about not having water and wanted Windy to leave. So Peggy Ann loaded their belongings on a caravan of mules and headed for San Francisco. She hoped it would be better there. But it was about the same, maybe even a little bit worse.

One day Windy was blowing the clouds around. She took a deep breath and a piece of earth in the middle of California came right up off the ground. It left a place lower than the ocean. People called that place Death Valley.

All that dirt and rock ended up in Windy's mouth. Windy didn't want to swallow it, so she blew it into the ocean, making some new islands. The sea birds didn't mind at all. It gave them a place to nest and rest. The whales liked playing tag around the islands.

The people in San Francisco were afraid Windy would inhale all of California one day and blow it to China, or some other faraway place. There was another town meeting. The people decided Windy had to be exiled from California for good.

Windy climbed on Peggy Ann's lap and kissed her good-by. "Don't worry," she said, "I'm old enough to take care of myself." Peggy Ann had to agree it was true.

With one mighty breath, Windy took in all the clouds and air she could. Round as a balloon, she floated up to the sky. She sailed off with a flock of geese heading south.

Peggy Ann couldn't bear being away from Windy all the time. She moved to an island and built herself a lighthouse. There Windy could visit her from time to time and not bother anyone.

As for Windy, she floats around with the clouds most of the time. Whenever there's a hurricane, people know it's just Windy playing with a little rain and wind. If they catch sight of Windy playing tag with the clouds, they run for cover. She's sure to stir up a batch of tornadoes.

Of course, now that Windy is older, she's always looking to do good deeds. Whenever Peggy Ann sights a ship in trouble, she signals Windy to blow the ship safely to port. It looks as if taking care of all the ships will keep Windy and Peggy Ann busy until the sea goes dry.